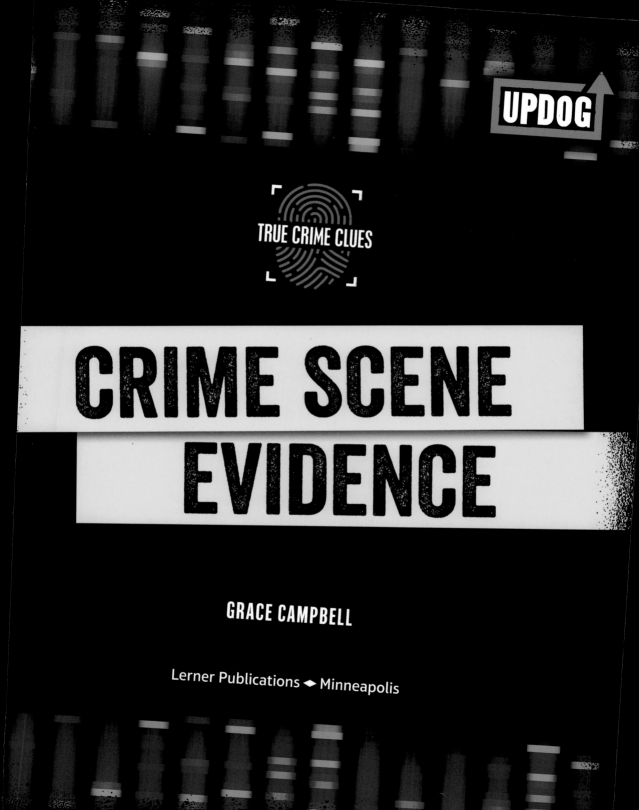

UPDOG

TRUE CRIME CLUES

CRIME SCENE
EVIDENCE

GRACE CAMPBELL

Lerner Publications ◆ Minneapolis

EVIDENCE

Lerner Publications Company
An imprint of Lerner Publishing Group, Inc.
241 First Avenue North
Minneapolis, MN 55401 USA

For reading levels and more information, look up this title at www.lernerbooks.com.

Main body text set in ITC Franklin Gothic Std.
Typeface provided by International Typeface Corp.

Library of Congress Cataloging-in-Publication Data

Names: Campbell, Grace, 1993– author.
Title: Crime scene evidence / Grace Campbell.
Description: Minneapolis : Lerner Publications, [2021] | Series: True crime clues (UpDog Books) | Includes bibliographical references and index. | Audience: Ages 8–13. | Audience: Grades 4–6. | Summary: "When investigators enter a crime scene, everything is considered evidence. Find out how to preserve the scene and collect the evidence"— Provided by publisher.
Identifiers: LCCN 2019039959 (print) | LCCN 2019039960 (ebook) | ISBN 9781541590571 (library binding) | ISBN 9781728401362 (ebook)
Subjects: LCSH: Crime scene searches—Juvenile literature. | Evidence, Criminal—Juvenile literature. | Forensic sciences—Juvenile literature.
Classification: LCC HV8073.8 .C358 2021 (print) | LCC HV8073.8 (ebook) | DDC 363.25/2—dc23

LC record available at https://lccn.loc.gov/2019039959
LC ebook record available at https://lccn.loc.gov/2019039960

Manufactured in the United States of America
1-47576-48106-12/11/2019

CONTENTS

Fingerprint Powder

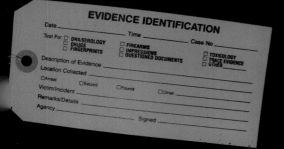

EVIDENCE IDENTIFICATION

Date _____ Time _____
Test For ☐ DNA/SEROLOGY ☐ FIREARMS   Case No _____
☐ DRUGS ☐ IMPRESSIONS
☐ FINGERPRINTS ☐ QUESTIONED DOCUMENTS   ☐ TOXICOLOGY
  ☐ TRACE EVIDENCE
  ☐ OTHER _____
Description of Evidence _____
Location Collected _____
☐ Arrest ☐ Seized ☐ Found ☐ Other _____
Victim/Incident _____
Remarks/Details _____
Agency _____
_____ Signed _____

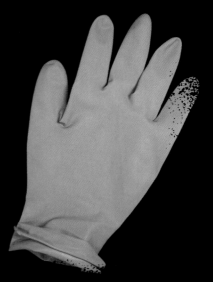

WHAT IS CRIME SCENE EVIDENCE?

Detectives arrive at the scene of a crime.
They'll need to find evidence to solve it!

crime: an illegal
activity

evidence: something
that investigators use
to prove a theory

Detectives use evidence
to find their suspects.

suspects: people who may
have committed a crime

DNA is a type of evidence that can be collected.

DNA: material in cells that carries genetic information

Fingerprints, hair, and blood are examples
of DNA evidence.

Physical evidence such as broken glass, weapons, or clothing often has DNA evidence on it.

Investigators store away the evidence they find at crime scenes.

UP NEXT!

EVIDENCE SOLVES A COLD CASE.

POLICE LINE DO NOT CROSS · POLICE LINE DO NOT CROSS · POLICE LINE DO NOT CROSS · POL

cold case: an unsolved criminal investigation

CASE BREAK!

A cold case from 1995 left detectives with nothing but blood-splattered rocks. In 2013, technology was able to read the DNA. Cold case solved!

UP NEXT!

EVIDENCE IS CAREFULLY COLLECTED.

ROSS

POLICE LINE DO NOT CROSS

POLICE LINE DO NOT CROSS

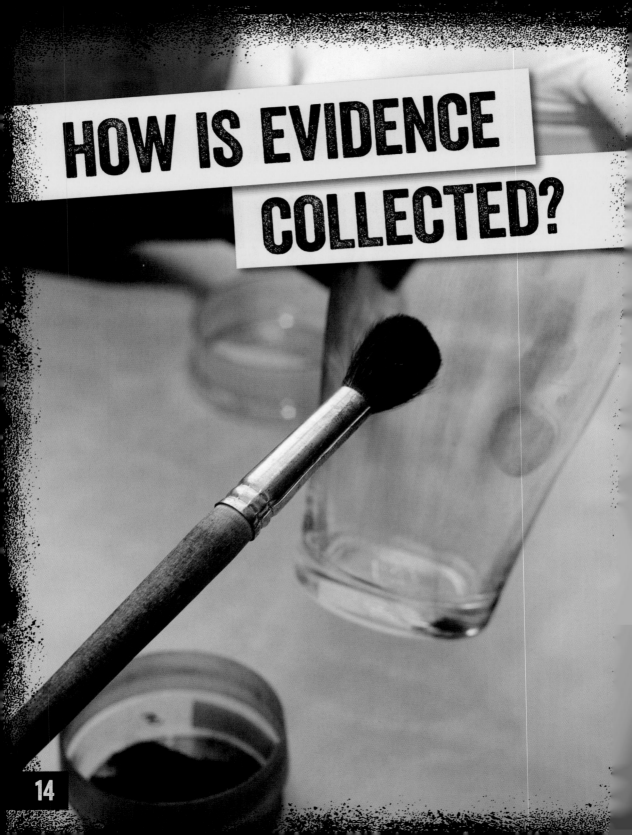

HOW IS EVIDENCE COLLECTED?

Investigators wear special uniforms when collecting evidence. They take pictures before they carefully bag and label evidence for lab analysis.

investigators: people who solve problems by observing closely

YOU'RE THE DETECTIVE

You are at the scene of a robbery. The suspect left behind a piece of chewed gum. It will probably have the suspect's DNA on it. Detective, how should this gum be collected?

A. photographed, then bagged and labeled
B. bagged, then photographed
C. photographed and left in place

Answer: A. photographed, then bagged and labeled. Then you can remember where it came from when you bring it to the lab for testing.

UP NEXT!

TAKING EVIDENCE TO COURT.

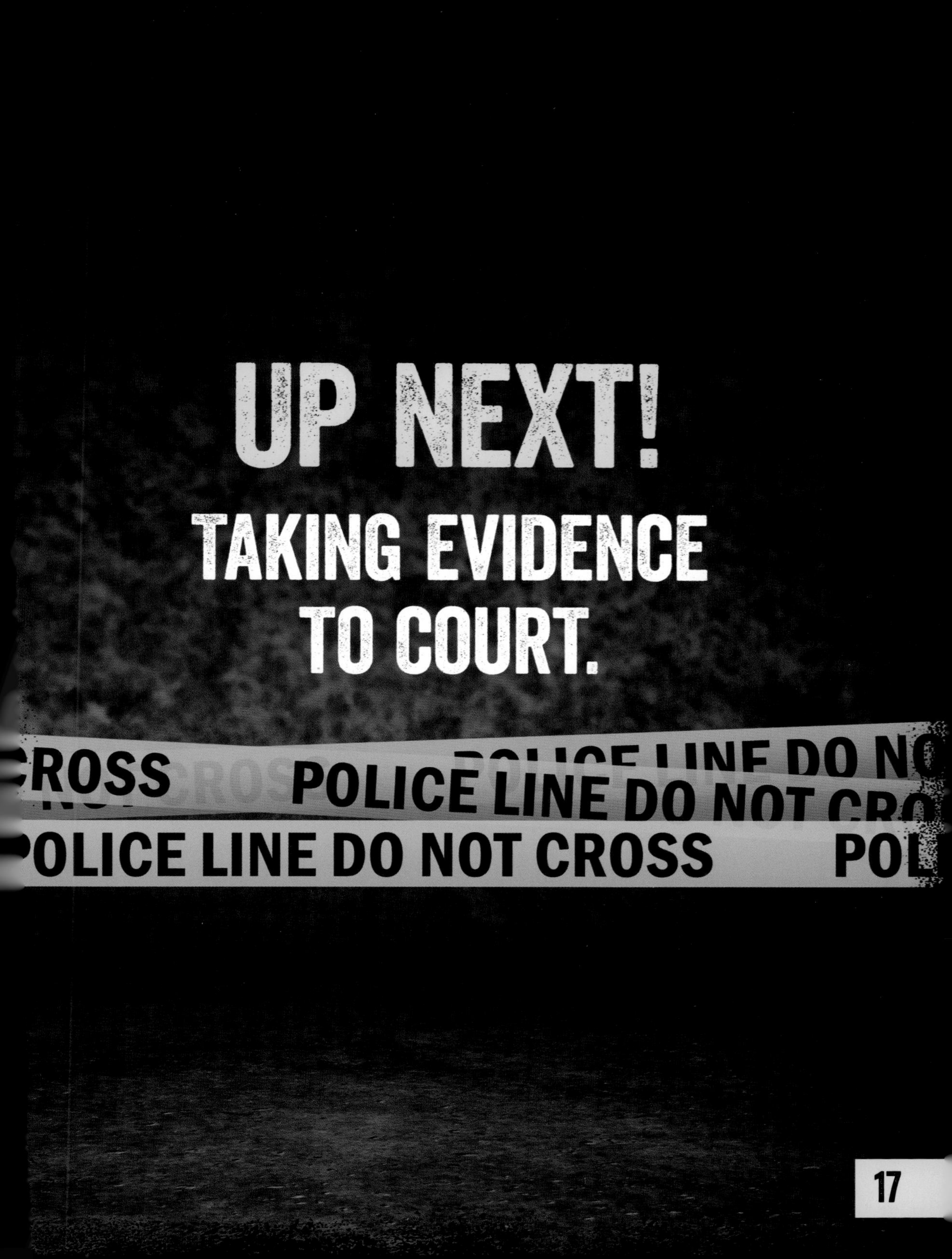

POLICE LINE DO NOT CROSS

POLICE LINE DO NOT CROSS

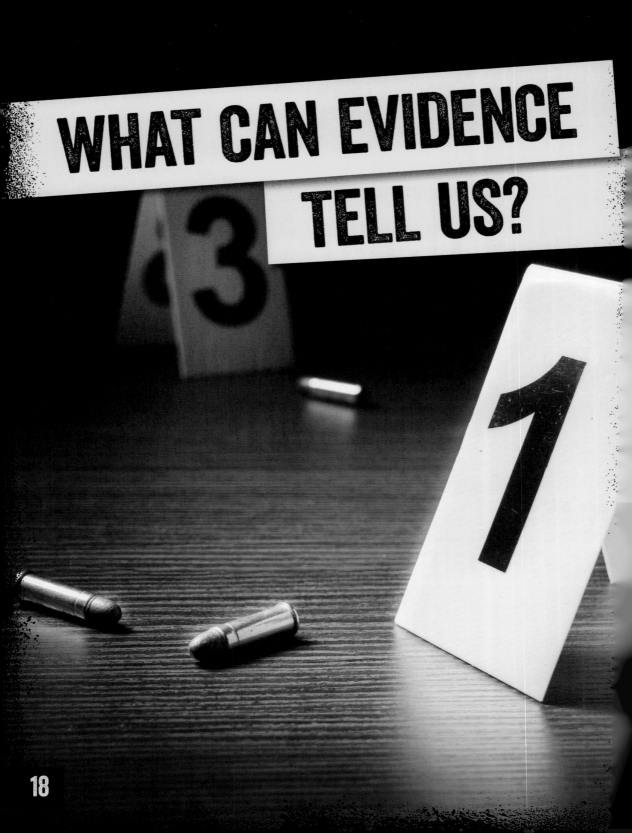

WHAT CAN EVIDENCE TELL US?

It can take a long time to bring a case to court. Preserving evidence is important. Detectives could need it years later.

Contaminated evidence can keep a criminal out of jail.

contaminated:
damaged or ruined

Strong evidence can help a lawyer convict the suspect.

GLOSSARY

cold case: an unsolved criminal investigation

contaminated: damaged or ruined

convict: to find or prove to be guilty

crime: an illegal activity

DNA: material in cells that carries genetic information

evidence: something that investigators use to prove a theory

investigators: people who solve problems by observing closely

suspects: people who may have committed a crime

CHECK IT OUT!

Adventures of Cyberbee
http://www.cyberbee.com/whodunnit/crimescenenonflash2
_sites.html
Solve the crime of the Barefoot Burglar.

Campbell, Grace. *Blood Evidence.* Minneapolis: Lerner Publications, 2021.
Learn about the science of blood evidence and how it solves crimes.

Hunter, William. *Mark & Trace Analysis.* Philadelphia: Mason Crest, 2014.
Find out about all the types of evidence and how investigators work with them.

Orr, Tamra. *Investigating a Crime Scene.* Ann Arbor, MI: Cherry Lake, 2014.
Learn more about how pros investigate crime scenes.

Science News for Students
https://www.sciencenewsforstudents.org/article/crime-lab
Discover all the ways that forensics are at work in our lives.

Sutinis, Beth. *Crime Scene Techs!* Broomall, PA: Mason Crest, 2016.
Learn what investigators look for at crime scenes.

Wood, Alix. *Killer Evidence: Be a Police Detective.* New York: Gareth Stevens, 2018.
Get a more in-depth look at the work detectives do.

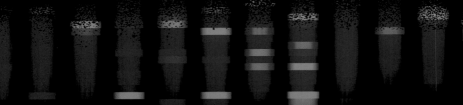

INDEX

PHOTO ACKNOWLEDGMENTS

Image credits: Digital Storm/Shutterstock.com, p. 4; D-Keine/E+/Getty Images, p. 5; Tetra Images/Getty Images, p. 6; CIPhotos/Getty Images, p. 7 (top); Svisio/iStock /Getty Images, p. 7 (bottom); whitemay/E+/Getty Images, p. 8; Tetra images RF/Getty Images, p. 9; Westend61/Getty Images, p. 12; diy13/ Shutterstock.com, p. 12; franz12/Shutterstock.com, p. 14; stevanovicigor/Getty Images, pp. 15, 16 (background); Grumpy59/Getty Images, p. 16; Fer Gregory/ Shutterstock.com, p. 18; dcdebs/Getty Images, p. 19; Microgen/Shutterstock .com, p. 20; Image Source/Getty Images, p. 21. Design elements: ktsimage/ Getty Images; ulimi/Getty Images; jamesjames2541; ABDESIGN/Getty Images; stevanovicigor/Getty Images.

Cover: digicomphoto/Getty Images.